THE INCREDIBLE AND MIGHTY *Soya Bean*

Phenomenal Product with Total Life Style Changes

CYNTHIA LOGAN

AuthorHouse™ LLC
1663 Liberty Drive
Bloomington, IN 47403
www.authorhouse.com
Phone: 1-800-839-8640

Published by AuthorHouse 03/11/2014

ISBN: 978-1-4918-7026-6 (sc)
ISBN: 978-1-4918-7035-8 (e)

Library of Congress Control Number: 2014904353

authorHOUSE®

CONTENTS

Dedication Page

This book is dedicated to my husband, Howard, my constant source of encouragement while writing this book; and to my devoted children, Haydn, the patient and supportive photographer, and Charise, whose help, understanding, and confidence in me, spurred me on to the book's completion.

ACKNOWLEDGMENTS

To my many friends, loved ones, and colleagues, I owe a mountain of appreciation and gratitude. Their ears are often fatigued by my inappeasable desire to present an excellent book.

I am especially grateful to my friend, Yohko Hirromatsu for adding a professional touch to my book, by facilitating my review in the delivery of my food images.

I thank God for you all and for the privilege of sharing this book with you.

Getting the most from this book

This little book about the Soya bean is both exciting and informative. It is written to alert its readers to the realization that small things which are widely appreciated, and highly acclaimed for virtues, should never be taken for granted nor underestimated for their worth. From this small and seemingly insignificant legume, lies the potential for great and powerful acts that can change personal lives, and impact the course of history forever. Soy bean is greatly appreciated for the incredible contribution it has made to 21st century health advancement, yet the amazement it has caused to health proponents in staggering. How amazing that the soya bean (Glycine Max), a native legume of Southeast Asia, now grows abundantly in America with more than a dozen varieties, and is responsible for a large percentage of economic gain as a major cash crop. With outstanding properties of phytic and alpha-linden acid and isoflavones, the soy bean oil is the main resulting ingredient. Further, many products have been generated with the oil. Be advised, and it is encouraging to learn, that the wonder product, ***Bio Diesel*** is brought to view with astounding significance. Biodiesel is America's first Advanced Bio-fuel, and a renewable, clean burning diesel replacement. Do you know how important this is to the United States? Has it occurred to you how its contribution impacts our economic growth? This renewable clean burning diesel replacement is actually reducing the dependence that United States has on imported petroleum. You will come to realize that today, with technological advancement, there are innumerable soy applications derived from the soy bean; food, industrial products and even drugs.

Most of these provide dependable industrial alternatives. It may interest you to note further that among the list are adhesives, coatings, printing inks, lubricants, plastics and specialty products. Because of the many benefits achieved from soy products, plans are underway to increase soybean demand through advancements in soy-based research and technology. Soy bean offers versatility for many applications, and opens the door for a variety of uses. An important consideration is the division of soy components during processing into soy protein (soybean meal) incorporated into many human foods, and soy oil, some of which is applied in industrial applications. Wow! We can read and we must research. By engaging in diligent information search, we can certainly discover soy's incredibility for ourselves.

The health claims about the humble soybean are allegedly beneficial in the following areas.

- ✓ Soy has high protein content and soy products can provide a significant portion of a person's daily protein needs.
- ✓ Soy helps to prevent Cancer of the Breasts, Prostrate, Colon and Uterus.
- ✓ Soy helps to prevent Heart disease and in some cases may help to prevent disease by reducing cholesterol.
- ✓ Soy may help to prevent Osteoporosis or alleviate menopausal symptoms.

The health conscious, on the other hand, take seriously, the simple and direct claim that Soy is not good for human consumption unless it is fermented. Many heated controversies are also connected to this direct claim. As a consequence, it would be beneficial for all of us to grasp the nature of the controversies and plan what each of us can to do to address them. Although we may be locked into new ways of thinking, relentlessly, we should determine to participate in this tight ideological battle. This should help shape our minds and improve our economy in preparation for overcoming the struggles of many health issues, while maintaining a healthy lifestyle. We can start with personal research and check the facts for ourselves; especially because food entrepreneurs have turned consumers on to soy by claiming soy ingredients are not only safe but beneficial. But studies are showing that there is a dark side of soy which has existed with us for many, many years. So, even for small things or occurrences, there is need for enquiry and research, awareness for changes in our lives, and acceptance or rejection from the powers that be, depending on certain prevailing beneficial influences. However, soybean farming and soybean production are here to stay. Hence, it is worthwhile to be constant and conscientious about follow-up on anything and everything that impacts our lives and wellbeing. The Soya Bean is one such consideration, so let all be involved.

At the end of each chapter, there is a statement which reflects the importance and significance of the Soya bean as it impacts our lives and our world today.

INTRODUCTION

I considered writing about Soy bean for three reasons:

Firstly, I made myself a promise to learn as much as I could about this soya bean, simply because I love Tofu and was enamored by my first introduction to this new food product. I accepted the notion that this food would prove a high protein addition to my diet and would help to forego or stall any appearance of certain dreaded diseases. I consider this Soya Bean a significant Change Agent for the 21st century.

Secondly, the progress and usefulness of the Soya Bean has been phenomenal. It is interesting to learn of the history and progress of this little bean; its historical background, growth, and influence, its widespread popularity and how much it has impacted the life style and eating habits of the world around us. As a people interested in change and progress, you and I should know about these accolades. But this will happen only when we personally make the effort to be more inquisitive and pro active about our interests in the factors of our society. The humble little bean has been used in myriads of ways to produce various items both in the food industries and non-food industries. Food-industry estimates believe that a large percentage of processed foods add bulk, flavor and texture to their products. Pharmaceuticals, health advocates, farmers, ordinary consumers, and leaders engaged in agricultural expansion in many countries are now using this little bean as a life-saving staple for many of their peoples. There seems to be no limit for the usefulness of the humble soya bean, when creative and innovative energy via technology is used for its development. From the production of biodiesel oil, irritants, coagulants, toys, medication for certain diseases, contraceptives, and myriads of versatile product, the soy bean has been used to make these items a reality.

Thirdly, many issues have been raised about Soy bean and the production of Soya food production, in relation to our health. It would seem as if soy foods appeared out of nowhere to be regarded as a "miracle health food" in our 21st century. Soya has taken over the world. Is this a good thing and do we as consumers benefit? More people need to know and be made aware of the prevailing criticisms, benefits, dangers and risks. Does this super food, soya bean, pose a serious health risk to us? Should the Soy food products be eaten, or can they be eaten in small portions? These are questions we need to answer and facts we need to know and verify. There should be no fear of voicing our opinions because any question raised about our health and well being is pertinent to our happiness. Specific new ideas discussed in this book will include soy benefits and health issues, and how we should honestly and openly approach the subject. It is hoped that readers will do personal research and investigation, in an effort to be more knowledgeable and adaptable to the importance and truthfulness of all such allegations, as well as knowing the benefits to be gained from using the Soya bean and its consumer and industrial products.

CHAPTER ONE

Small Wonder—Incredible Origin

Do you like beans? Well, if you do, then you'll like Soybean; In the United States it is officially known as the soybean, while in the United Kingdom it is known as soya bean, acknowledged and written as two words. (1) With its genus name classification, Glycine Max, it is a species of legume, and a native of East Asia. It was given the name, Glycine Max because of the unusually large nitrogen-producing nodules on its roots. (2) The soybean plant has been classified by the UN Food and Agricultural Organization (FAO) as an oilseed rather than a pulse. Among the many wonders of nature, this simple little vegetable has grown for its edible bean which has numerous uses. Further, "the soy bean has been discovered to be a crop of long domestication, having a cultural variety with a very large number of cultivars" (3). A further classification of the Soya bean is that *Glycine Max* is officially accepted as the domesticated bean, while the wild soy bean is referred to as *Glycine Soja*. They have been given two species names because their uses and characteristics are very different. Technically they are of the same species.

With its distinctive origin and history, the soya bean has drawn many admirers as well as critics. (4) Discoveries of the Soya bean are revealed by (Gibson, L and Benson, G, 2005). "The first domestication of soya bean has been traced to the eastern half of North China in the eleventh century B.C. or perhaps a bit earlier." Soy Bean certainly was an important staple, fit to be in company with other foods of its kind such as rice, wheat barley and millet. The Soya bean has its own unique and intriguing history and some of these are here mentioned. (5) "The first use of the word soybean in the U.S. literature was in 1804, and for many years the soybeans were used as a forage crop rather than harvested for seed"

Production of the soy bean thrived initially in Pennsylvania, as it appeared to be well adapted to the soy composition. Seed varieties of Soybean to the United States were brought from Japan and harvested at two agricultural experiment stations in New Jersey. It was George Washington Carver who first experimented with Soybean and other nitrogen-producing legumes to find new uses for the crops. He developed more than 300 by-products, including oils and food substitutes. His work led to the development of Soybeans' two main uses in America – the edible oil and meal. Soya bean production gradually expanded into the U.S. Corn Belt and its major turning was in the 1940s, up to and after World Wars I and II. American farmers and soybean processors were ready to fill the gap caused by China and World War II, when they disrupted Soybeans production and put traditional sources of protein and oil in short supply. (6) From a special report given by the SOY-INFO center, (Shurtleff W; Aoyagu, A. (2007) reveals startling progress of soybean production in major areas of the U.S. "The dizzying rise of American soybean production during World War II exceeded even the wildest expectations of . . . the crop more than doubled during the war and increased an astounding 77% (from 106 – 188 million bushels) during the single year 1941-1942)" Today's production from more states far exceeds this percentage. A multiplier effect prevailed in the early 1950s when soybean meal became available as a low cost, high protein feed ingredient. This triggered an explosion in the American livestock and poultry production, which led to an assurance of a vast and continuing market for soybeans farmers output. But what is more exiting is the fact that the U.S. soy exports have also grown steadily with insatiable needs and demands both inside and outside of the United States. Allegedly, Soya bean is today's America's third largest in cash crops. The Soy bean feed is beyond human comprehension. Alongside the growing production and uses, is the important factor of growing incomes among citizens. In many other countries such as China, Egypt, Indonesia, Mexico, the Phillipines, and Russia, Syria and Vietnam there is an increase in the disposable income of many people and this results in higher living standards.

So, if you like new and exotic things, whether that turns out to be food, clothing, building items, candles, engine oils, flooring, furniture, ink, personal care items, stain removers, toys, waxes; or if you want to be a customer in unique areas of industrial functionality areas such as biodiesel by engine manufacturers, or even about car companies that use soy based form in their seats then you'll definitely like soybean. Soy bean has changed the world, people's choices, and the way of life of many people, in extremely marvelous ways.

And if you're interested in engaging in campaigning with consumers, interested in emerging markets which promise success for new and exciting products, then, go ahead, and purchase new soy products without hesitation. You're in for a treat. All types of people are making personal discoveries that there are many more uses for soy products than has been revealed to the public has been revealed. Be bold and creative, buy new clothes just for fun and novelty, be inquisitive and experiment with new foods and products, and there's no doubt, soy bean will be a best-seller for you. Tell any of your friends or acquaintances that you can both envision change and accept the portrayal of bringing great and marvelous changes into existence, and there is your second reason for appreciating soy bean. This little miracle vegetable, soybean, will lead you to navigate in the roughest seas, just so you can accept the marvels that this little wonder has brought to our planet earth. You'll simply appreciate Its nutrients alongside its variety and usage.

Samuel Bowen, a sailor who located America in 1765 introduced the most versatile farming product the earth has seen: the soybean

CHAPTER TWO

A Preponderance of Soy bean Foodstuffs

Although we have taken it for granted, the amazing soya bean can be processed into many healthy foodstuffs that people can appreciate. Many people have come to know the many products of Soy and are confidently using them with frequency. For convenience, these foodstuffs can be categorized accordingly:

Vegetarian Diets: Soy beans can be easily processed to resemble other foods. They are now widely used in meat and dairy substitutes. Today there are many varieties of soy milk, soy butter, soy yoghurt, soy ice cream, soy cheese available in many supermarkets. There are meat substitutes such as veggie burgers, soy hot dogs, soy bacon that are becoming increasingly popular. Many vegetarians use Tofu and Tempeh as the major protein sources in their diet.

Fermented Soybean Products are utilized as condiments, especially in Chinese cuisine; Whether as packaged food or as ingredients in the processing of food, soy is now a favorite and a specialty in the fermentation process. Fermented Soy Bean Paste, Soy Sauce, Natto and Tempeh are outstanding products by fermentation. Natto is a natural favorite in Indonesia, where the soya is fermented by bacteria. For Tempeh, the soybeans are fermented by fungus.

Fat-free (defatted) soybean meal is a cheap source of protein in many pre-packaged meals and in some animal feeds.

Traditional non-fermented food uses of Soya beans include Soy Sauce, Soy Milk, and from the latter, tofu and tofu skin. A variety of milkshakes, smoothies with fruits and Cream is now being introduced, and found to be healthful for lessening weight for the conscious weight watcher.

Biscuits, Cookies, Health bars, Protein bars and Soy nuts (or baked soy nuts) are sumptuous favorites. Besides the traditional snacks, there is also a new wave of soy products carried by some famous distributors. To name a few, there is the Soy dream for milk, Soy Protein Isolate, and Soy Beans Toasted and Salted, Soy Roasted beans, as well as croutons.

Textured vegetable protein (TVP) are ingredients in many meat and dairy analogues such as Burgers, Hot dogs, Bacon, Sausages and Mincemeat.

Soy Bean Oil and Soy Meal Soybean oil is used in many processed foods, and it is also used as a fixative for other essential oils in cosmetic and insect-repellent products. In the production of soybean oil, the discarded husks of the soybean are used to make soybean meal, which is a major source of animal feed in the United States. A large percentage of soya bean grown in the United States is used for this purpose.

Roasted Soybeans produce candies, confectionary, cookie and cracker ingredient, cookie topping, dietary items, soy coffee and soy nut butter and soy nuts.

Using all the aforementioned products from soy bean can certainly excite us. But wait! There are many people who do not know of the myriads of benefits of soy bean. However, as time progresses more and more products are being created from soy bean, and there is great potentiality for many more with multiple benefits to be been attained.

Below are listed food uses for Whole Soy bean Products. Baked soy beans produce with full fat flour, Bread, Doughnut mix, frozen desserts, Instant milk drinks, Low-cost gruels, Pancake flour, Pan grease extender, Pie crust, and sweet goods.

Here's a definitive question for you? Have you ever thought about using complete Soybean Meal Products for your meals? There are scores of these Soy bean products to be considered. Grits, soy flour, concentrates and isolates are significant considerations. Infant formula, bakery ingredient, beer and ale, candy products, cereals, confections, diet food products, meat products, noodles, prepared mixes, sausage casings, special diet foods and yeast, and lots more to be considered. The green soy beans also known as Edamame, is now a popular consumer delight. They are harvested prematurely while the beans are still green and can be quickly preserved and frozen so that their fresh, sweet flavor can be retained. The Edamame are available throughout the year, and can be kept for several months. They can be found in many Asian markets. Interestingly, Edamame was first a popular food in Asia, but has now become very popular in many other countries around the world.

From the SEED of the soy bean, Soy Sprouts are germinated and used for human consumption. Because these soybeans are high in protein, they are also used as a major ingredient in livestock feeds.

Soya bean is essentially the most versatile plant the world has observed. Mankind can therefore access an array of relatively reasonable products.

CHAPTER THREE

Soybean produces Industrial Non-Food Items

Soybean Lecithin Products for Industrial Uses

The engaging little Soybean is now recognized as a multi-market producer of various items for diversified use. Soybeans non-food items, are used extensively in industrial products, including oils, soap, cosmetics, resins, plastics, inks, crayons, solvents, and clothing.

Soybean oil is the primary source of a diverse variety of resources, including recycled cooking oils, and animal fats for making Biodiesel in the United States. " Biodiesel is a renewable, clean burning diesel replacement, which reduces the United States dependence on foreign petroleum, job creation and environmental improvement" (7) From (Biodiesel Basics, 2013). Further, it has been claimed that "Biodiesel is the only commercial-scale U.S. fuel produced nationwide to meet the advanced criteria of the EPA agency According to EPA, "biodiesel reduces greenhouse gas emissions by at least 57 percent and up to 86 percent when compared to petroleum diesel"

Soybeans have also been used since 2001 as fermenting stock in the manufacture of a brand of Vodka as fermenting stock in the manufacture of a brand of vodka. (8) The Vodka is usually made from potatoes or grain, but soy beans, grapes or sugar beets may be used, even though less common.

All commercially available steroids start with soy sterols. It is noteworthy to learn that the soybean is now the prime source of steroidal drugs, including contraceptives and steroidal anti-inflammatory drugs.

Henry Ford promoted the soybean, helping to develop uses for it in food and industrial products. He went as far as demonstrating auto body parts made of soy-based plastic. Ford's further interest was to make a Soybean car, so for each one; he was inspired to use two bushels of soybeans with other products for their completion. He was also instrumental in making the first commercial soy milk, ice cream, and all-vegetable non-dairy whipped topping.

In 1936, Ford Motor Company developed a method where soybeans and fibers were rolled together producing a soup which was then pressed into ingredients to make new products. This took place just before and during World War I, when innovation and industrialization were employed to push agricultural and manufactured growth. There was a growing thirst for new things and a hub of activities for new uses of old raw materials, and entirely new substances that could change the focus of the world. Today, various markets are expanding because of the resurgence of new soy products. Our seemingly unassuming soy has essential and mighty properties for the propagation of many and varied products. (9) Much research according to (Russell, J, 1942) reveals that "manufacturers began to look at cotton, oil, coal, wood, peanuts, soy beans and other natural products, not as raw materials in themselves, but as compounds of raw materials. In the United States, Soy beans, is one such natural material which has been used as a base for cellulose products on an annual basis. In passing, (Russell, J, 1942) further stated that, "The Soybean Car, also known as the Hemp Body car was a concept car. Its first iteration of the body was made partially from Hemp and Soybeans" Today, very high quality textile fibers are made commercially from "Okara" (soy pulp, a by-product of tofu production. (10) Car ingredients for the soybean car were composed of:

"Frame: made of tubular steel, attached to fourteen plastic panels. (1/4" thick

Windows: made of acrylic sheets. This led to a reduction in weight from 2500 pounds car to a 1900 pounds car, a 25% reduction in weight.

Plastic ingredients, speculated to be a combination of soybeans, wheat, hemp, flax and ramie."

Anti—Foaming agents: Soy is embedded in the manufacture of Alcohol and Anti-spattering agent such as Margarine manufacture. For Dispersing agents, there is Ink manufacture, insecticides, paint manufacture, pigments (paint) and rubber manufacture.. The incredible little soy bean is also involved in many more produces for industrial uses.

Refined Soybean Oil Products – Industrial Uses

Anti-corrosive agents, Anti-static agents, Caulking compounds, Core Oils, Diesel Fuel, Disinfectants, Dust Control agents, Electrical Insulation, Epoxies, Fungicides, Herbicides, Inks, printing, Insecticides, Linoleum backing, Metal, casting/working, Oiled fabrics, Paints, Pesticides, Plasticizers, Protective Coatings, Putty, Soaps/Shampoo/detergents, Vinyl Plastics, Waterproof cement and Wallboard.

A close-up look on soy shows that the bran (hulls) of all seeds and legumes contain substances called *Lignin.* The highest level of lignin is found in soybeans. *(*11) "Soy Lignin is a complex organic polymer found in the tissues of plants. Lignin plays a crucial part in conducting water in plant stems. It also plays an important role in the carbon cycle, sequestering atmospheric carbon into living tissues of woody perennial vegetation". The significance of this lignin compound must not be underestimated as its unique properties have been used for many and varied uses in production. This highly lignified wood is durable and therefore a good raw material for many applications. . "Lignin is also one of the most slowly decomposing components of dead vegetation contributing to a major fraction of the material that becomes humus as it decomposes." One can therefore appreciate its economic significance in making newsprint, Kraft processes, excellent fuel value, and plastic injection molding." We can take a look at a few of its involvement as a soybean.

"In 2007, Lignin extracted from shrubby willow was successfully used to produce polyurethane foam. (a)

In 2012, it was shown carbon fiber can be produced from lignin instead of from fossil oil, (b) In 2013, the Flemish Institute for Biotechnology was supervising a trial of 448 poplar trees genetically engineered to produce less lignin so that they would be more suitable for conversion into bio-fuels." ©

When Henry Ford, one of the finest of America's businessman made the Soybean Car, he was looking to integrate Industry with Agriculture

CHAPTER FOUR

Science Comes Alive with Soybean Breakthrough

When I consider the fame and usefulness of the soy bean, two great idioms come to my mind. "Good gifts are wrapped in small packages" and "whatever is worth having is worth working for". For soy bean this is just as pertinent as all other important things in our lives. In the late 1939 and early 1940s, Soya Bean made a big breakthrough which now benefits the world at large. (12) As cited from (Science Alive, 1940-1953) "After an accident involving one of the large soybean oil storage tanks at the Glidden Company, the renowned chemist Percy Julian, at the workplace, unexpectedly discovered and revealed a new method for producing large amounts of *stigmasterol* from soybeans". It is explicitly stated that:

"Stigmasterol is a steroid, a class of chemical compounds that includes the sex hormones and several other human hormones. Because stigmasterol was in the same family as other hormones, it could be used as a starting material from which to make other hormones. One such hormone was progesterone, a female sex hormone that was important in helping pregnant women avoid miscarriages."

Julian enlarged the process of synthesizing progesterone from *Stigmasterol* and converted it to Progesterone in bulk. This method was successful, but Julian the Industrial chemist persisted in making big changes in the segregated world then. In 1948 scientists at the famous Clinic in Minnesota discovered that the human hormone was good for treating arthritis, a disease of the joints in humans. For a second time, the master chemist started the idea at Glidden to make a change for cortisone.

As further cited in (Science Alive, 1940-1953). "Julian read about it and realized it was a steroid, which could be easily converted to cortisone. In 1948 Julian published a process of synthesizing Reichstein's compound S from a relatively common compound called 16-dehydropregnenolone. It immediately increased the production and reduced the price of cortisone and remains one of the most inexpensive ways of making this important chemical today".

The first major product was *progesterone* and then it really blossomed out with the second, *cortisone.* Actually, the development of Lecithin granules, a substance extracted from Soybean and a food supplement was the first product that Julian made while at the Glidden Soya Division. The second was a fire-retardant called Aerofoam, widely used by the navy during World War ll. Julian created a wide variety of soy-based products while at the Glidden Soya Division. This young chemist's work experiences and research at the Glidden Company, prior to his big discovery in the 1940s had prepared him for these exciting and masterful accomplishments, the discovery of developing large amounts of stigmasterol from soybeans, and cortisone. Progressively his second feat, an astounding breakthrough, was that of discovering cortisone, and making it affordable for arthritic patients. This inventor of new uses, enamored with the soya bean, made an industry out of the simple soya bean. (13) (Science Alive, 1936—1939—Julian Perry) makes it very clear that a chemist's success came from unprecedented personal efforts.

Never underestimate the value of small things. Small things have great power both for good and evil.

CHAPTER FIVE

Soya bean Impacts the World's Eating habits and Life style Changes

Are you the type of person who likes to add new and exciting foods to your diet? Do you like preparing new recipes which promise greater nutrition and better taste? Have you ever experimented with natural foods such as nuts, grains, fruits and vegetables, instead of the traditionally prepared refined foods? It might interest you to know that foods such as peas, beans, a variety of nuts, fruits and vegetables, when added to meals and eaten in their natural state, promote health, improve physical beauty and add variety to meals.

Would you ever consider changing your eating habits from animal foods to becoming a vegetarian? You might wonder whether or not your daily protein requirements would be satisfied, or whether you would long for the taste of meat from animals. If you have been thinking about these things, then you are not alone. Many Americans and people from all over the world are now carefully and deliberately changing their style of eating, and choosing the quality of their food intake. Not only is this consideration intriguing, it can also be sensible and healthful. Most people have chosen tofu, one of the biggest soy food products, soy milk, preferably unsweetened, Soy beans, Tempeh, Miso, Edamame and organics, as well as other vegetarian substitute products in their diet plan. You too may decide in favor of this change. In doing so, be well advised on this choice.

May I introduce you to a delectable, naturally nutritious and economical food, the versatile salt free, sugar free, non-cholesterol, high-quality protein substitute – TOFU! or "bean curd a moist product made from the curds of Soya Bean. The process is similar to that of making cheese. Tofu is made from coagulating soymilk and then the resulting curd is pressed into soft white blocks.

To preserve its moistness, it must be kept in water, especially when refrigerated. USDA certified organic Tofu are made with only Non-GMO Project verified Soybeans. Nasoya Tofu is available in a variety of textures, Soft/silken tofu, Firm and extra Firm. Organic, non GMO Tofu is the best brand for you. It can help you make a healthy change in your diet by increasing your protein intake while reducing fat and cholesterol. Tofu has very little flavor or smell of its own. This allows it to be very accommodative and can be prepared either in savory or sweet dishes, because of its bland background.

For a period of time Tofu was primarily the choice of Vegan substitutes for meat. There was a common misconception that vegetarians do not get as much protein as meat lovers do. The truth is that some vegetables have all of the essential amino acids that your body requires, even though vegetables are composed mainly of carbohydrates. By choosing certain vegetables and adding them with Tofu in preparing a meal, wholesome and healthy protein to the body can be provided. It has been discovered though, that you have to eat more tofu, than you would meat protein in order to meet the recommended dietary protein levels.

Because Tofu originated in China and is presently consumed in both eastern and western countries, there are myriads of dishes that have been tried and tested that can be enjoyed when preparing this food item. However, today this boneless meat is consumed in many countries, and gourmet cooks has adapted a particular way of preparing delicious Tofu delicacies. In my own preference, I have adopted many of the western methods of preparing Tofu. Tofu is considered a delicious and nutritive delight, and revered as a number one soy bean food product.

Authentic sources inform us that Tofu is one of the greatest and most complete of protein foods. On the American diet and nutrition list, Tofu joined the ranks of new and exciting foods, approximately 40 years ago. Although a relative newcomer, it is accepted as a highly competitive mainstream protein substitute especially for vegetarians, because it generates improved nutrition, is of immense value as an economic contributor, and because of its versatility in meal creation. To enhance the nutritive value of Tofu, you can combine it with other complementary foods, such as other beans, nuts, fruits and vegetables, with flavors of your choice.

Besides Tofu, numerous soy products for both food usages as well as for industrial purposes are now widely marketed in the competitive soy market. Soy is therefore good news for vegetarians, big business for pioneer small businesses, great upstarts for creative enterprises, big profits for pharmaceuticals and economical satisfaction for the ordinary man in the street. The Soy business has mushroomed into many parts of the United States and other countries and recently the market for other soy food products, especially the fermented ones is rapidly increasing.

With big changes in the eating habits of many people, soy meat, along with many non-soy food products are now becoming popular substitutes and can now be found in different brands and varieties. These products are rapidly replacing Tofu, as a secondary source of meat for vegetarians. People who like creating delightful dishes can find a variety of meat substitutes in various soy products. The following soy products are listed as recommendation and delight in cooking.

Light-life Gimme Lean Vegetarian Ground Sausage. This product is made from textured Soy protein and taste and smell like sausage. You can prepare it according to your liking, but it can be fried easily and added to others dishes

Morning—Star Tomato and Basil Pizza burger. This is a vegetable burger made from soy protein and has a unique flavor. This frozen burger tastes like Pizza and has pieces of Mozzarella cheese baked right into it. They are so delicious; they can even be eaten as little nuggets.

Worthington Vegetable Skallops or (Scallops) may be found in your local health food store. Worthington, a division of Morning Star farms, makes a very large variety of canned imitation meat products. This is also a Soy and wheat protein product, essentially low in fat and calories. With these scallops you can increase your creating in making a variety of tasty dishes and nuggets.

Boca Italian Meatless Sausage is also made from soya protein, and come in packs of four, Find it in the freezer section of large supermarkets. Italians seem to love sausage and meatballs in sauce as a favorite dish. If you particularly want to try going the Italian way, you can try these and see how well you appreciate Italian cuisine. This protein soy product will fry like sausage links and add flavor to the sauce.

Frieda's Soyrizo. This product is the Spanish vegetarian sausage, a precooked soy based meat alternative having the delicious flavoring of Mexican chorizo. They can be found in the produce section of large supermarkets and if you are lucky, you may find them at Wal-Mart!

Frieda's Soyrizo is a high quality with a distinctive flavor, and is a soy textured protein. The meat is stuffed inside plastic casing similar to real chorizo, but is 100% vegetarian and gluten free. The casing must be removed before cooking. For people who love rice and beans, chilies and tacos, here's the chance to be truly creative.

Soya bean food products have penetrated the eating habits of the entire world, and lifestyles will never be the same as before.

CHAPTER SIX

Background Specs of Soya Bean

Formerly, the Soy bean from which Tofu is made was an imported crop from South West Asia, India, or Argentina. Today, however, it grows extensively in other countries, where both warm and cold climates prevail. Today's cultivated soybean plants have undergone years of domestication of careful selection during more than 30 centuries. Primitive farmer-breeders then were known to selectively keep the larger seeds from year to year to replant, in the hope of increasing their yields and the total weight of food harvested per acre of land. This method involved creating a plant with more erect growth habit, less shattering of the seeds, and less twining (all of which facilitate harvesting, especially by machine)" To further appreciate plant characteristics of the soybean four basic concepts have to be understood. These are: (i) Photoperiodism, (ii) Maturity Groups, (iii) Vegetable Types, and (iv) Determinate/Indeterminate Soy Bean.

Photoperiodism refers to how flowering plants respond to changes in daily, seasonal, or yearly cycles of light and darkness. Plants need to know when to produce flowers, so that seed development can be accomplished before the next winter arrives. (14) Uniquely, "Soybeans, as legumes contain a built-in time clock. Their flowering and ripening is controlled by the length of day and night, the photoperiod, instead of Air temperature".

Maturity Groups refer to a classification of some crop varieties, especially soybeans, and their growth and development. As an example, soybean with a maturity group 0 to 00 needs only a short growing season before harvest; whereas, a soybean with maturity grout V or VI needs a longer growing season before the plant is completely developed and ready for harvest. There are 13 Soybean Maturity Groups ranging from 000, 00, 0, I, II, III, IV, V, VI, VII, VIII, IX, X. (14a) "Soybeans grown in Canada and the Northern parts of US are classified as Maturity Group 00 and 0 respectively. Those grown in the central US belong to Maturity Group II through IV. Those adapted to tropical and sub-tropical zones are classified as Maturity Group IX and X. Varieties suited to the northern maturity groups mature quickly, in about 80 – 90 days after planting. Those in the southern warm climates take longer, 100 – 150 days"

(14b) "Vegetable Type Soybeans are also called edible or garden type soybeans. These were introduced to the US in 1980. They are larger seeded, somewhat better tasting, and easier to cook and shell than field type soybeans".

"An Indeterminate soybean plant continues to grow and put on new leaves and nodes at the top of the plant while at the same time, the plant sets flowers and pods at the bottom of the plant." (14c) It has been observed that presently, all commercial soybeans grown in the northern latitudes of (MG 00 through IV have an indeterminate growth habit. This is encouraging news for soybean farmers. Supply will be ahead of demand in most places. With increased harvesting of soybeans, there are always more gains in marketing, as well as production. Greater yields in harvesting, proves that there is also a huge advantage of indeterminate soybeans over determinate varieties is the fact that they can recuperate faster periods of dry weather. Encouraging!

Fermentation of soybean products has attracted many customers to eating soy, so Tofu lovers are now moving towards eating soy in a fermented manner. This growing tendency has proven healthy and nutritious to many people. (15) "Fermentation of soybean products requires yeast, bacteria, mold or a combination of each. Usage of bacteria, mold and yeast, gives the fermented food a special flavor, texture, and aroma"

Additionally, fermentation preserves food, improves digestion, by breaking down proteins within various foods, and it also enriches substrates with nutritional essentials such as vitamins, amino acids, and fatty acids. For many years, the Chinese have used the fermentation process to transform soybean into various types of soy foods such as soy paste, soy sauce, sufu, a type of cheese, and stinky tofu. The good news is that other countries have gradually adopted the soybean fermentation habit from the Chinese. Some identified food derivatives are Miso, Tempeh, Natto, Hananatto, and Hawaijar. As cited by McGee. H, (2004), "Preservation of foods, specifically in a brine (fermentation of these products uses a high salt content) is how many of these products were discovered when soy bean instead of meat or fish were used most likely during the vegetarian Buddhism movement".

As an added accomplishment, Soybeans are also described as another of the biotech foods, meaning that the crops have been genetically modified by the soybean farmers. The claim is, it is good news because it helps people around the world eat healthier. But technically speaking, is it really true for soy bean?. (16) From research findings, (Thomas, P and Earl, R. (1994) have stated that "Current biotechnology methods allows the transfer of gene from one organism to another" This is not unusual as this method is basically like the process of crossbreeding and fermentation, and have been used for centuries to increase crop productivity, improve food supply and produce better foods. For further emphasis, it is alleged that, "Biotechnology helps the entire world eat healthier. It allows farmers to grow the enhanced soybeans that produce the improved oils we enjoy today. For example, biotechnology helped create trans-fat free oils and soybean oils enriched with omega-3. It prevents crop devastation, helping to ensure that people all around the world have enough to eat. And it allows soybean crops to be grown with significantly less pesticides".

Another use for the soybean is that the soy protein can be good substitutes for animal products as well. A new functionality is now underway for the demand for global aquaculture for new customers.

Full-fat soy beans, soybean cakes, and soybean meal are the most commonly used soy products in feeds in aqua-culture species. Other soy products are being tested for future usage.

CHAPTER SEVEN

TOFU, Introduction to the Bean Curd

I'll never forget the day I first encountered Tofu. By invitation, I joined my high school friend and her mom for dinner, and devoured a sumptuous meal, followed with great fun and past reminiscences. The white boneless meat was among the mouth-watering fare I ate. It was a delicious and appetizing meal. I complemented her cooking and admitted that I had never eaten that meat before. She smiled acceptingly and responded with a surprise "That's TOFU. You've never had it before?" After hearing my apologetic response, she excitedly gave me a quick pep talk about this Tofu, how healthy it was, and hastened to inform me where I could buy it for myself.

My friend's last reminder to me before we parted was exciting. 'Remember to buy the Tofu. You'll find it in the supermarket. It looks like cheese'. She further added that I could cook it easily and prepare it the way I wanted, because Tofu accommodates any flavor to which it is added. I was eager, excited, and intrigued and I smiled silently, pondering 'TOFU here I come!' Being a health freak, highly conscious and supportive of nutrition and wellness, as well as being an aspiring gourmet cook, any food offering the novelty of naturalness, freshness and wellness is welcome in my cuisine collection. Further I especially wanted to impress my husband and friends with "WOW" dishes. So off I went to shop for this new food – Tofu, for added nutrition and wellness to my cuisine collection.

Thoughts of lovely dishes of Tofu, displayed on my dining table, raced through my mind. However, that did not materialize very quickly because finding the Tofu was a difficult exercise for me. I needed to know more of the history of Tofu and how it was made. I began to wonder what information had I missed, or was I not looking carefully enough for this tofu? I didn't even know then, that it was made from bean curd. Neither did I know it was preserved and packaged in water. I didn't even know there were different types and consistencies of Tofu. But I did learn it was a highly nutritious vegetarian protein. Thumbs up! Nutrition was involved. I gave up the search on my first attempt to find Tofu.

I resumed my research as soon as I left the supermarket. After all the research was completed, I did find the Tofu and it did look like a block of cheese. I learnt many other things too. Some people, especially Asians made it on their own and sold it locally both in supermarkets and in the regular ground provision section of many large super markets. The Tofu is easily identified because it is packaged in water to keep it fresh. My early encounter relating to Tofu and my eager research for knowledge of Tofu took place, a few years back. Since that time, I have discovered much more about Tofu, its improvement and versatility, and have made many favorite dishes as my *Tofu Dishes with a Difference* and displayed them with pride.

Authentic sources inform us that Tofu is one of the greatest and most complete of protein foods, on the American diet and nutrition list, Tofu joined the ranks of new and exciting foods, approximately 40 years ago. Although a relative newcomer, it is accepted as a highly competitive mainstream protein substitute especially for vegetarians, because of its versatility, nutritive value and its economy. To enhance the nutritive value of Tofu, you can combine it with other complementary foods, such as beans, nuts, fruits and vegetables, with flavors of your choice.

Here's to sharing one of my favorites:

Tofu Egg Salad from (17) Nasoya Recipe

INGREDIENTS:

- 2 lbs firm Tofu ½ cup soy mayonnaise of regular mayonnaise
- 3 tablespoons Dijon Mustard ½ teaspoon turmeric
- 1 tablespoon cayenne pepper 2 tablespoons chopped parsley
- 1 tablespoon chopped fresh dill of dried dill
- ½ cup green onions
- Dash of salt and pepper

DIRECTIONS:

- Drain Tofu
- Cut into quarters, then wrap thickly in paper towels on a cutting board.
- Weigh down the wrapped Tofu with heavy canned goods to get out excess water
- Let sit in refrigerator for 10-20 minutes.
- Mash Tofu in bowl with a wooden spoon
- Mix Tofu well with remaining ingredients
- Chill and serve.

All's well that ends well. There's a lot of common sense gained, as well as alertness practiced in health principles, while preparing Tofu Dishes with a Difference.

CHAPTER 8

Dishes with a Difference and Tips for cooking
Soft Oatmeal and Tofu Cookies

INGREDIENTS:

- 1 block 16 ounce Firm Tofu
- 1 Cup Oatmeal
- 3 tablespoons Organic Ketchup
- 2 tablespoons brown sugar or honey
- ½ cup Soya milk
- 1 tablespoon soy sauce
- 3 tablespoons whole wheat flour
- ½ cup chopped onions

- 1 tablespoon coconut oil
- 1/2 teaspoon sage
- ½ teaspoon cumin
- 1 cup slivered almonds
- ½ cup Chopped celery
- 2 tablespoons lemon juice
- ½ cup bread crumbs
- 1 tablespoon vanilla

METHOD:

- Line a baking sheet with parchment paper and spray with cooking spray.

- Preheat oven to 350 degrees.

- Press small pieces of Tofu through strainer to get rid of some of excess water. When all is done, place tofu in a large bowl, add salt and crush finely.

- Saute` onions and celery in coconut oil and add to tofu mixture.

- Mix oatmeal with ketchup, sugar and lemon juice.

- Add dry seasoning, nutritional yeast, and carrot into mixture with soy sauce and stir thoroughly.

- Add flour, milk, and vanilla and gradually combine all ingredients, into mixture.

- Shape into soft and flexible dough.

- Form into small cookies and bake for 30 minutes, turning them after 15 minutes to add brown evenness to both sides. Your cookies are ready to cool, then eaten. Enjoy!

Cooking Tips:

Spread bread crumbs evenly on the cutting board. Use a wooden spoon to scoop out cookie amount and attempt equal portions for cookie sizes. Form each cookie by patting dough in your hand, and then patting each one in the bread crumbs coating.

Always use a little lemon juice in your mixture. This will make your dough soft and flexible.

DELICIOUS TOFU OATMEAL COOKIES

INGREDIENTS FOR
TOFU BERRY SMOOTHIE

- 1 block soft or silken Tofu
- ½—1 ripe Banana, ½ cup strawberries
- ½ cup raspberries or blackberries
- 1 cup fresh orange juice
- ½ cup blueberries
- 1/2 cup soy milk, 1 6-oz packet of yoghurt and a pinch of nutmeg
- Smoothies will require other ingredients, such as fruit for flavoring.

TOFU BERRY SMOOTHIE

METHOD:

Blend all the fruits, yogurt and milk with the Tofu and orange juice, in your Vita Mix blender or other recommended blender. This smoothie will be tangy and sweet because of the berries mixed with the orange juice. Enjoy!

These fruits may also be used for other smoothies combination with Tofu.

Yoghurt, milk, orange juice and silken Tofu used for Tofu Berry Smoothie

SCRAMBLED TOFU – A delicious and simple Breakfast fare

INGREDIENTS:

- 1 lb. firm tofu 1 red bell pepper, finely chopped
- 1 carrot finely grated
- 1 stalk of celery finely chopped
- 1 small tomato finely chopped
- 1 small onion finely chopped
- 1 teaspoon cayenne pepper
- 1 teaspoon cumin
- 1 tablespoon soy sauce
- 2 tablespoons olive oil or coconut oil.

METHOD:

- Squeeze water out of tofu
- In a large bowl, mash tofu well with fork
- Add onions, pepper, celery, salt, and carrots and mix well.
- Add soy sauce and dry seasoning, and thoroughly mix with other over high heat in a large saucepan and pour your tofu mixture in.
- Scramble, like you would seasoned egg. Sprinkle in a pinch of salt to your taste.
- Lower heat and scramble until golden brown.
- Serve warm with toast or muffin and enjoy.

Research all claims about SOY, and "HEALTH PRODUCTS' before serving them to your family

CHAPTER NINE

Soya and Health – Benefits or Disaster

We have been introduced to the wonders and marvels of soy. Its virtues have been highly extolled, yet its impact on our health is taken lightly, or brushed aside as propaganda. Soya is a food that many vegans eat regularly because it is considered by many agencies to be a source of complete protein. (18) (Lee, 2006) asserts that, "Soy contains the full complement of amino acids, can be made to fit with a low fat diet" Although this is good news especially for vegetarians and vegans or even for people wanting to reduce the amount of meat intake in their diet, this can be a cautionary tale. Long before I was aware of the benefits of fermentation, I was always cooking my Tofu delights and adding various vegetables, fruits, nuts and spicy seasonings to make a difference, because I am a believer of a balanced diet and an advocate for healthy living.

There is the added proponent that Asians eat a lot of soy and are very healthy. This is not altogether true. One wonders whether a red flag isn't being waved in your direction. It has been shown that Asian diet include fermented soy beans of Natto, Miso, Tamari and Tempeh, Further discovery shows that the Japanese and Chinese eat very small portions of fermented soy per day, and usually as a condiment. Strangely, though, even without the consumer's knowledge, Soy is found in most supermarket breads, in imitation meat, and dairy products like milk cream, cheese, yoghurt, and ice cream and most importantly, soy is found even in infant formulas. It would seem that manufacturers recommend and entice the American public to consume more Soya than the Japanese consumers.. The fallacy is evident here. Certainly there is a belief that 'too much of one food is unfit for human consumption'. Some truth is told here in the issue of health and wellness. Too much soy in a person's diet can be detrimental to a person's health.

Here are some common allegations about soy, and we can ponder whether these are fact or fiction.

Tofu was first used in monasteries in China 2,000 years ago, in part to promote sexual abstinence, since the phytoestrogens in soy can lower testosterone level. Except in times of famine, tofu was only used as a condiment, with pork, seafood and other forms of protein being preferred.

The soymilk we drink today is highly processed food, full of toxins as well as additives to make it palatable. However, (19) research shown by (John Henkel, 2007) strongly attest that "Recently raised concerns focus on specific components of soy, such as the soy isoflavones diadzein and genistein, and not the whole food or intact soy protein:

Soymilk is not the "health food" it is promoted to be.

The "miracle health food" has been linked to brain damage and breast cancer

SAD. Standard American Diet contains too much soy. Americans eat soy mostly in unfermented forms, which are made into various processed imitation foods.

High levels of phytic acid in soy reduce assimilation of calcium, magnesium, copper, iron and zinc. High phytate diets have caused growth problems in children.

Trypsin inhibitors in soy interfere with protein digestion and may cause pancreatic disorders. In test animals soy containing trypsin inhibitors caused stunted growth.

MSG a potent neurotoxin is formed during soy food processing and additional amounts are added to many soy foods.

Soy foods increase the body's requirement for Vitamin D.

Fragile proteins are denatured during high temperature processing to make soy protein isolate and textured vegetable protein.

Are you frightened by any of these allegations? Perhaps you should be. Have you been led to thinking that the unfermented and processed soy products are good for you? If you are, then perhaps we can question whether or not soy products, including soy based infant formula may be major contributing factors to all types of diseases. This is another claim. Let's further cogitate? If you are experiencing unusual weight gain, bloating and/or nausea, could it be eliminated just by removing soy products from your diet? This can be doable, but it will take discipline and determination. Do you believe it is a coincidence that today's families are seeing many more cases of obesity, thyroid problems, osteoporosis, cancer and many more diseases than our ancestors?

There are many other allegations on the benefits and risks of Soy. Yet in spite of these allegations, people are finding new uses for soybean. Do you consider this growth as attributable to a massive shift in attitudes about soy? Let's think more deeply. The attitude shift was the result of intensive investment in advertising by the soy industry and it was highly successful. But for these, we have to make some decisions for ourselves. The American public has been confused and misled for too long. The course for action is that, as consumers, we must educate ourselves, be strong, and do our own research and while doing these, apply some common sense. Since the consumption of soy products is rapidly increasing, the clarity on the benefits or hazards of these products should be considered as well, and the unresolved health issues must undoubtedly be addressed. We have been thrown into this soy world for the long haul, and we have to fight relentlessly to win this battle. For the benefit of health and wellness, let's concern ourselves on areas of positive participation. A major way to begin moving forward in our involvement would be to work interactively with the Food and Drug Administration.

After all shouldn't the foods that consumers purchase be tested and regulated? Of course! This public domain, as required by the law, publishes regulations of many kinds of agency actions in the Federal Register. Federal regulations are either required or authorized by statute. Some regulations address specific problems or known health hazard. Other procedures address citizen petition regulation deemed as administrative or procedural. So why not exploit the authenticity of this area of public safety and accountability? (20) In its agenda of Regulation, the FDA sets up a regulatory information system. The process most often used is the NRPM, the Notice of Proposed Rule Making. Procedurally, it is specific and straightforward. "The proposed rule explains what we intend to require, or intend to do, as well as our basis, (e.g. scientific and policy reasons) and asks for public comment. Comments are generally submitted via the Federal government's electronic docket site, available at Regulations.gov. So as consumers we can have a say, and we can know what food items are safe and unsafe for human consumption. Further there is a way to know what policies and regulations are enacted since we can contribute our concerns via comments by invitation.

The final rule explains the regulatory requirements (also known as the "codified" portion), the impact of these requirements on industry or the public, and responds to the comments on the proposed rule. These regulatory requirements, or codified portion of the final rule, also are published under Title 21 of Code of Federal Regulations.

Why don't we consider using this communication to query our own health issues?

Perhaps there will be no clear and honest answers because of the concentration and emphasis of large profits for the soy industry and impaired health for most people deceived into using unfermented soy for the long term.

As more and more is learned about the biological activity of these isoflavones, concerns are raised as to whether they are harmful or helpful. It is the attention which is focused on soya bean isoflavones, and the associated class of phytoestrogens that is disconcerting. (21) As described by a noteworthy Dietician, (Hood, S., 2006) "the most notable concerns are around infants consuming soya, and women with oestrogen positive breast tumor. Evaluating the health benefits of phytoestrogens is complex as these compounds have been shown to have many different effects. The problem comes when trying to determine whether it is safe to eat Soy, and if so, just how much. Do we truly have an answer to the question of soy being paradoxical? Can a product promoted to be so good for our health really be that dangerous and devastating? Then maybe, we should pause before we take another bite of tofu or take another gulp of the delicious soy milk. Study after study has linked the Asian wonder bean to the relief of menopausal symptoms, lower cholesterol levels, and the prevention of cancer and bone disease. What confusion! This can prove discouraging. Should we then abandon Soy? One set of people claim existing danger in consumption of the soya bean and its many food products, yet another set defend its benefits and advocate its propagation. The answers are complicated but we have to find them. One thing is certain, we cannot change the past, but we have an opportunity to be actively and positively vibrant about our future every day. We can make informed decisions and educated choices for ourselves.

A lot of vegetarians and lactose-intolerant people turn to soy foods for healthy nutrients, because, soy foods are considered good protein and calcium sources.

Certain Soy Health myths allege that Asians eat very little soy products, and ultimately live longer and healthier lives. But can we prove how many grams are eaten at one sitting? It may be true that the amount of soy that Asians consume is far less than Americans, and that American vegans do substitute Tofu as their meat substitute on a large scale, but the key to Asian's healthy diet is moderation. Most Asians take some fermented soy as condiments with their meals and also add a lot of varied foodstuffs such as seaweeds, vegetables and rice.

Fermented soy is safe and healthy soy, and people are proponents of soy as a healthy food for the following reasons:

It is a rich source of Non-meat protein and calcium.

It lowers LDL cholesterol or bad cholesterol.

It produces Isoflavones (a compound in soy), and reduces the risk of initial and recurring breast cancer. But with all the fanfare of Soy and its healthy properties, as well as the acclaimed benefits it offers, many people think, and strongly believe that soy is unhealthy for food because:

It impairs thyroid function. (Soy may impact you if you have a thyroid dysfunction – just avoid)

Unfermented soy prevents protein and nutritional absorption due to phytic acid and trypsin inhibitors.

It causes mental degradation due to aluminum absorbed in soy. It is unfortunate that we don't have answers for all the claims and questions about soy but we CAN take steps to improve our health as related to soy.

"Soy is not a fad. It's a continuing trend that's here with us for the long haul."

CHAPTER TEN

Addressing the Claims of Soya and Health Issues

Some people should avoid Soy. Others should take it in moderation. Soya beans are not perfect food, and it has been said repeatedly there are a number of negative health effects which are associated with their consumption. The advice is, that soy food products should be consumed as part of a varied diet, and for the most part fermented soy should be used. Take your pick, which of these common usages will you pause to consider more deeply?

Let's make a comparison here. If you have maintained a friendship with someone for many years and there is a strong bond of trust between you both, and further, if your friend is an honest-hearted person whom you fully trust, would you take advice especially about health issues from that friend? I believe that it is highly probable. In the same manner and with the same fervency, consumers have developed deep confidence in the advice given by health authorities and advocates to the public and they still do. Hence, this is the reason, when it comes to Soy, consumers have put much confidence into lawmakers, health advocates and even manufacturers when it comes to foods as it pertains to health. On the other hand, sales of soy products aren't declining, and soy bean farming is increasing in great proportions. The soy industry has even stepped up its marketing of products all over the word.

(22) As cited by (Daniel, K., 2008) "the bottom line is that the safety of soy foods and formula has yet to be proven and that people eating large quantities of soy are unwittingly participating in a large, uncontrolled and basically unmonitored, human experiment." Many governments around the world, Health Clinics, and Health Advocates, Institutes of Risk Assessment, Nutritional labs specializing in Food Sensitivity, University Research Programs specializing in Environmental Risk factors have all warned the public about the dangers of excessive soy food consumption. The claims before mentioned have great truth and the warnings should be heeded. Here's advice which pertains to Soy and your health-related issues.

Make and keep a Soy Alphabet diary. Know and follow your alphabet for safety and better health. Here's my contribution to the diary.

Accept the truth about the dangers and dark side of soy and work on withdrawal of unfermented soy products. Anti-nutrients are natural toxins found in soy. Some of these factors interfere with the enzymes you need to digest protein.

Be aware, be conscious, be knowledgeable, and be open-minded about Soy. Learn as much as you can from different intelligent sources. Buy Soy Foods that are labeled Organic.

Check labels to see if it contains soy. The Food Allergen Labeling and Consumer Protection Act of January 2004 requires that food manufacturers list soy on the label, because It's one of the top eight food allergens. Soy must be clearly stated on labels. Consume Soy in moderation.

Drinking even two glasses of GMO soymilk daily for one month provides enough compounds to alter a woman's menstrual cycle. The embedded soy antinutrients are quite potent. Much scarier is the fact that on a higher magnitude, infants fed with soy-based formula have estrogen circulating through their bodies.

Enzymes are anti-nutrients in unfermented Soy.

Fermented Soy is the safest and best way to eat soy. Tempeh, Miso, Natto and Soy Sauce are all traditional fermented soy products.

Genetically modified (GMO) crop is greatest in soy within the United States. The process is engineered by Monsanto, a chemical company for the benefit of enhancing sales of their huge Billion dollar money machine. A high percentage of soy grown in the US is genetically modified. GM Soy has been linked to an increase in allergies.

Hemagglutinin is a clot-promoting substance that causes your red blood cells to clump together. Soy contains hemagglutinin. These clumped cells are unable to properly absorb and distribute oxygen to your tissues.

Improve your thought patterns concerning how to digest foods. Listen to your "gut" instincts.

Judge for yourself, the shattering ill effects of soy after reviewing thousands of studies published on soy, the incredible and mighty bean.

Keep a numeric count of the health benefits of the soy bean.

Learn how to recognize and manage your diet without ingesting unfermented soy. Listen to your "gut" instincts.

Menopause: For some women there is evidence that soy's isoflavones improve symptoms of menopause, hot flashes. For others it worsens the symptoms. MSG is a potent neurotoxin. It is formed during soy food processing, and is also a mask for soy's unpleasant taste.

"Natto" has been given high marks as a fermented soy product because of the major benefits it offers. It is considered the best food source of vitamin K2. (23) Research on (Mercola.com, 2010) shows that "Vitamin K2 is essential to preventing osteoporosis, cardiovascular disease, and diseases of the brain such as dementia, and protecting you from various cancers including prostate, lung, liver cancer and leukemia."

Organic products that are certified cannot intentionally be made with artificial ingredients. They are not allowed to utilize any GMO ingredients.

Phytoestrogens are produced by leguminous plants but is most concentrated in Soy and is slightly different from the estrogen hormone produced by the human body.

Question the "Silk" products. Soy Milk leaves you comfortable about the product. Silk uses NON-GMO Soy beans. The product is without genetic engineering. The beans are selected only of high quality without genetic engineering right here in North America. Silk products manufacturers believe "that the less you mess with mother nature, the better"

Research! Research! Research! Get the facts for yourself. Read labels to be sure you are ingesting the best.

Soybeans are processed (by acid washing) in aluminum tanks, which can leach high levels of aluminum into the final soy product.

Take responsibility of your own health and stay positive. Thousands of studies link soy to malnutrition, and many health challenges such digestive distress, immune system breakdown, thyroid dysfunction, and reproductive disorders and infertility.

Unfermented Soy is unfit for consumption. It has been linked to digestive distress, immune system breakdown, high risk of heart diseases and cancer. Using soy as the only protein source in your diet is a bad idea.

Vegetarians eating a high soy diet are among the groups that experience very high negative effective from the anti-nutrient properties of soy.

Whenever soy proponents argue in favor of soy-based foods, they actually lump together the fermented with the unfermented products and then claim the benefits and protection that these products offer.

'eXpect' opposition and denial of clear facts regarding the dark side of soy from soy proponents. But you can receive support and validation of the truth about soy in its relation to health from health conscious individuals and organizations.

You really do not have to be on the Soy bandwagon. What you need to be is open-minded, knowledgeable, and keep researching. It is hardly likely that you'll ever get the full story unless you research it for yourself. So do the research. It's simple. You WILL find the answers. Then go ahead, make your decision and stay on the road marked safety. You can leave the Soy alone or be a soy-fermented moderate.

Zero tolerance for unwholesome and questionable foods is the watchword for developing healthy bodies without unfermented soy consumption.

The AHA, American Heart Association recommends that soy products be used in a diet that is varied.

BIBLIOGRAPHY

(1) (2) (3) Glycine Max, retrieved from http://en.wikipedia.org/wiki/Soyabean

(4) Gibson, L; Benson, G (2005) Origin, History and Uses of Soybean (Glycine Max) retrieved from http://agron-www-agron/iastate.edu/course/agron212/Readings/soy-history.htm

(5) Glycine Max, retrieved from http://enwikepedia.org/wiki/Glycine Max.

(6) Retrieved from http:///www.soyinfocenter.com/HSS/production

(7) Biodiesel Basics, retrieved from http://www.biodiesel.org/biodiesel—basics

(8) Environmental Protection Agency retrieved from http://enwikipedia.org/wiki/Soybeans/#other

(9) Russell, J. (1942) Synthetic Products and the Use of Soy Beans. Retrieved from http://www.jstor.org/discover/10.2307/141406

(10) The Soybean Car retrieved from http://enwikipedia.org/wiki/Soybean Car.

(11) Lignin,—an article about the Wood Polymer, retrieved from http://en.wikipedia.org/wiki/lignin

(12). Science Alive – Steroids from Soybean retrieved from http://www.chemheritage.org/Perry

Julian/history

(13) Science Alive: Becoming an Industrial Chemist: 1936—1939 retrieved from http://www.chemheritage.org/percy julian/teachers.

(14 a, b, c) Shurtleff, W; Aoyagi, A, (2001) Soy plant Botany, Nomenclature, Taxonomy, Domestication and Dissemination. Retrieved from http://www.soyinfocenter.com/HSS/soybean-plant1./php

(14d) Soybean and Corn Advisor, Inc. (2009—2013) retrieved from http://www.cornandsoybean.com/news/Feb 24_12_

(15) Fermentation of Soy bean Products. Retrieved from http://microbewiki.kenyon edu/index.php/soybean

(16) McGee, H. (2004). On Food and Cooking: The Science and Lore of the Kitchen.

(17) Nasoya recipes retrieved from http://www.Nasoya.com

(18) Lee, J. (2006) About Soy Foods, retrieved from http://www.johnleemd.com/store/soy.html.

(19) Henkel. J, 2007) Soy: Health Claims for Soy Protein. Retrieved from http://enhancedfp.com

Nutrition/soy-claim-soy

(20) FDA, US Food and Drug Administration, Protecting and Promoting Your Health, retrieved from http://www.fda.gov/Regulatory information/Rules Regulation

(21) Hood, S. (2006) Why Soybean is bad for you. Retrieved from http://www.optimumchoices.com/soy/htm

(22) Daniel, K, (2005) The Dark Side of America's favorite Health Food, retrieved from http://journal.livingfood..us/2011/09/06/soy-dar-side-of-a-healath food.

(23) Mercola.com (2010) The truth about Soy. Retrieved from http://www.articles.mercola.com/sites/articles/archives/201009/18/soy-can-dmage-your-health

ABOUT THE AUTHOR

Cynthia Logan is a native of the island country of Jamaica, West Indies, where she received her primary and secondary education. She completed three years of college education at Shortwood Teachers' College after graduating from High School. She began teaching in 1970, taught for two years, then enrolled at the University of the West Indies where she pursued her undergraduate degree, majoring in Economics. She has been a teacher on all levels of private and public education, and an Administrative Assistant in various areas of leadership in Jamaica, New York and Florida. In 1996, while working at Teachers Insurance Annuity Association –College Retirement Equities Fund she enrolled at New York University, and pursued a Masters degree with an emphasis in Business Teachers Education. She continued as Administrative Assistant in New York after graduation in 1998 and served as Teacher Assistant, years later in Florida. In 2013 she completed a certificate in Education at Jones International University, specializing in Corporate Training and Knowledge Management at the Instructor level. Prior to obtaining her masters degree, Mrs. Logan completed a certificate in writing for children and teenagers. She is determined to share her thoughts with colleagues, relatives and friends, plus a wide array of the reading public at a time she considered "appropriate", "relaxing" and "dynamic", while she continued to be an avid reader. She considers writing in various genres a stimulating adventure and her lifelong dream of writing in several genres has only just begun. She is presently retired from public employment but maintains continuous involvement in Women's ministries, as well as Home and Family enrichment activities. She resides in Everett, Washington with Howard, her ailing husband, and their adult children, Haydn, Aiza, and Charise. She also has an adorable grandson, Oswin Raymond.

Printed in the United States
By Bookmasters